"Specific behavioral laws are being discovered by social scientists that incredibly merge and integrate with biomagnetics and Einsteinian physics. Einstein searched his entire life for a Unified Field Theory, a super theory of the universe, but the quest eluded him. What he omitted from his search was the element of mind. When Freudian and behavioral psychologies are combined with Einsteinian physics and certain New Age concepts, astounding answers fall into place."
>   --- Ron Dalrymple, Ph.D.
>   Recent interview

What people are saying about this book:

"This is an expression so clear, so simple, so powerful; other self-knowledge books seem inarticulate. As a lifelong student in search of true spiritual maturity, I see an age-old wisdom...__laserized__ by Dr. Dalrymple for the perceptive mind which longs to see itself and its unimaginable power!! The potency of his message is so awesome, I wish only that I had written it!"
>   --- Ernest A. Leipold, M.D.
>   Physician/Composer
>   Maryland

"I loved this book! I couldn't put it down! Destined to be one of the world's great best sellers - here's what the self-help devotees have been searching for!"
>   --- Ms. Valerie Fogl
>   Corporate Credi
>   Washington, D.

"The intrinsic value of this book mirrors the depth of understanding of each individual who reads it, from the innocent to the knowing one, of the highly competitive business of life. It is a fascinating, energizing, delightful focusing on the true reality of an individual's growth. In today's language, it conveys the realities known throughout the ages of man's experience."
--- Mr. Richard D. Morse
Assistant Treasurer and Director
Rutgers University, New Jersey

*"Incredible! This book simplifies the workings of the human mind, while defying the imagination! The most important book of the 1990s, it leaves other New Age books in the dust of the **future past!** A brilliant synthesis of ideas...perfect for the serious student of psychology, business, home management, life, philosophy...you name it!"*
--- Ms. Barbara Kiehne
Marketing Consultant, Maryland

"I was so excited about reading this book, I read it in record time. The book reminds me of sculpting, of visualizing in detail and then recreating a positive form from a negative mass. The form that each person creates is different - we each create our own vision, often seeing what we want to see. Next, we each interpret the finished product differently, and this is all part of the creative process. The message of this book is very enjoyable and easy to relate to (paraphrased)."
--- Ms. Catherine Reta Marie Demack
Sculptress, Maryland

THE

INNER

MANAGER

MASTERING BUSINESS, HOME

AND SELF

Ron Dalrymple, Ph.D.

First Edition

Celestial Gifts Publishing
Chester, Maryland

THE INNER MANAGER

MASTERING BUSINESS, HOME AND SELF

by Ron Dalrymple, Ph.D.

Published by:

Celestial Gifts Publishing
Post Office Box 414
Chester, Maryland 21619 U.S.A.

Copyright © 1987, 1989 by Ron Dalrymple, Ph.D.
Cover Illustration Copyright Chris Panzer & Ron Dalrymple, Ph.D. 1989
Printed in the United States of America
Library of Congress Cataloging-in-Publication Data.
Dalrymple, Ron.
    The Inner Manager
    Mastering Business, Home and Self
    Includes bibliographical references.
1. Success in business.
2. Self-actualization (Psychology).
3. Self-help techniques.
I. Title.
HF5386.D16   1989   650.1'3   89-92088
ISBN 0-935882-03-0   Softcover

ABOUT THE AUTHOR

Dr. Ron Dalrymple is a licensed psychologist in Maryland with a special interest in the higher, little understood powers of the mind. Combining his clinical experiences with years of personal research in physics, topological mathematics and philosophical analyses of Eastern and Western origins, he has devised a meta-theoretical system of thought which attempts to integrate these disparate yet interwoven strains of creative imagination into a psychological yet philosophical treatise that provides novel insights to major life questions as well as practical approaches to everyday challenges and problem-solving.

These approaches can be applied to business, home and personal life management, affording the individual a greater repertoire of ideas and techniques with which to address life's difficulties.

However, in no way should these concepts be substituted for direct clinical intervention with a trained and licensed mental health professional should the circumstances warrant it, especially because of the possibility of misinterpretation and misapplication of these concepts.

These concepts are presented as a philosophical treatise, and are not to be construed in any way as advice-giving or as psychological interventions to be adopted by the consumer without consulting a licensed professional mental health expert.

ACKNOWLEDGEMENTS

In the creation of any project, we stand upon the shoulders of others. It is not possible to cite all the individuals who directly or indirectly contributed to the evolution of this project, but the author would like to thank the many teachers and guides who helped forge the matrix of ideas manifest in this work.

Special thanks to Dr. R.S. Clymer, Dr. Paul P. Ricchio, Dr. Gerald E. Poesnecker, Dr. Bruce Fretz, Dr. Stan Hunt, Dr. Jack Hursch, Dr. Paul Lowman and Dr. Herbert Blodgett for philosophical perspectives. Thanks to Mr. Dan Poynter for his helpful guidance in publishing and to Mr. Moulton Farnham for his judicious editing of the text.

Deep thanks to those who showed the author that love and intellect best flourish together, especially Norma Dalrymple, whose transcendence was foreshadowed by the imago.

TABLE OF CONTENTS

WARNING - DISCLAIMER

This book is designed to provide information and creative ideas relative to the subject matter covered. It is sold with the understanding that the publisher and author are not here engaged in rendering professional psychological services or consulting services of any kind. If professional psychological or other services are required, a competent professional should be sought.

It is not the purpose of this book to reprint or represent all the information or ideas pertaining to this subject matter, but rather complement, amplify and supplement other texts. For more information, see the references in the Appendix.

Self-development and starting one's own business are not get rich quick or fly-by-night schemes, but rather the end result of much time and work. Every effort has been made to make this book as thought-stimulating as possible, but it should be used only as a source of stimulation and insight, and not the ultimate resource on psychological procedures, concepts or issues. Other mental health professionals will present radically different views, and this work is in no way intended to usurp or contradict those divergent points of view.

The purpose of this book is to educate and entertain. The author and publisher shall have neither liability nor responsibility to any person or entity with respect to any loss or damage caused or alleged to be caused directly or indirectly by the information and ideas contained in this book.

WARNING - DISCLAIMER

THE QUEST

There was a young man who had a dream.

His dream was born one futile night, after years of working for others in different businesses. He had grown tired of the daily struggle, finding it as exhausting as it was pointless.

He resented laboring his sweat and muscle away for the benefit of others. He watched his employers grow rich while he slowly moved ahead. He was told to be patient, but he wasn't sure he could live that long.

His most recent employer made his mind up for him when demanding that the young man work his favorite holiday, leaving his wife and two children at home - alone.

Frustrated and depressed, the man returned to his residence late at night. His wife and children were asleep. Feeling isolated and empty, he sat up late, brooding over his life.

He had graduated from a good business school, but the breaks just hadn't come his way. He had watched other junior executives play games with the boss to get ahead, but he felt self-conscious and foolish acting roles he didn't feel.

Besides, he hated games, and he wasn't going to play them!

He thought about changing jobs, but something told him the same atmosphere might prevail at the next place of business. He rubbed his eyes, let out a sigh and thought about bed.

Then it hit him!

He would forget about working for others! He knew he had the brains and drive to run his own business, and had always wanted to work for himself. He began to get excited about the idea. It might be tough, but he would be his own boss, work his own hours and eventually pay himself what he deserved in wages. At last, he thought, I'll have a fair employer - myself.

Suddenly, his flash of inspiration darkened - he knew his venture would demand long hours and some financial risk, but...what if it ended in ruin?

His heart quickened. He couldn't fail his family. He took a deep breath, determined to never let that happen.

Despite the risk, he remained intrigued by the idea. After much thought, he began to develop a plan of action. He knew what he had to do.

He would search far and wide until finding the advice and insight he needed to launch his new enterprise.

The next morning, he discussed his plan with his wife. She tried to support him wholeheartedly, but he saw the subtle traces of fear in her eyes. He knew she loved him too much to dash his hopes. With every ounce of strength inside him, he resolved not to fail her or the children. He went to his old job with a new attitude, and arranged to take some personal leave days to begin his search.

The following day, he called countless executives for interviews, telling the men and women he wanted to start his own business and was looking for advice.

Some brushed him off. Others gave hollow advice and hung up on him. A few patronized him with nebulous platitudes. He was beginning to get discouraged, but something told him to keep trying.

Finally, he spoke to a man who had built his own business from scratch and was now a soaring success. Surprisingly friendly, the executive invited him to visit.

The young man went to see the older gentleman, and was delighted, if not a little nervous, to sit in the huge office overlooking the city. Windows surrounded them on all sides. The commanding view was breath-taking.

The furniture was elegant but spartan. Nothing wasted. Everything in balance. After he was seated, the young man fidgeted in his chair.

The elder studied the neophyte, then leaned over him, peering into his eyes. The shock of iron-gray hair framed the rugged features. Brilliant eyes burned from a still handsome face. The young man was at first uncomfortable, but a sense of serenity soon came over him.

When the executive spoke, his voice filled the room. "You seem to have a certain presence about you, young man. Tell me, why do you want to build your own business?"

The young man spoke easily, as if he were talking to a good friend. He revealed his dream, describing in detail his ambitions and his desire to help his family. The elder listened intently, his gaze piercing. The furry brows arched when he spoke. "I believe you are sincere in your desires. Tell me, what would you do with your wealth and power, should you obtain them?"

Shifting uncomfortably, the young man thought for a long time. At last he said, "Use it to help others."

The older businessman scrutinized him for a second, then broke into a broad smile. He shook the young man's hand. His voice took on a warm, embracing quality. "I will help you, my friend. I will send you to see one of the greatest businesspersons the world has ever produced. Little known, her power, knowledge and resolve have helped countless others. But always quietly, behind the scenes. I am certain she can help you."

Excited, the young man asked, "Who is she?"

Enigmatic, the elder replied, "Her name and address are on this card. I'll phone her and tell her you're coming. But I warn you - you must speak only the truth to her! Otherwise, she will not introduce you to The Inner Manager."

"The Inner Manager? Who is that?"

The executive would only smile.

Deciding to agree with these conditions, the young man thanked the elder and left. He found his way to the address on the card, discovering a beautiful work of architecture towering eight stories into the sky. The building was shaped like a cone and glistened with gold reflectant windows. Four arches flowed up the sides of the structure, coming to an apex above the penthouse suite on the top floor.

The young man caught his breath. He entered the building and approached the receptionist. She looked at him with the same intensity he noticed in the elder businessman, her eyes crystal clear and sparkling light. She directed him to the penthouse suite.

The young man took the silver glass elevator, watching the floor recede beneath him. He felt as though he were leaving something behind, but he wasn't sure what. He left the elevator and walked into a luxurious but lean office. It reminded him of the elder businessman's suite. Windows circled the entire office, giving a panorama of surrounding parks and buildings. Soft light filtered through the tinted glass.

An angular woman was seated behind a desk that was shaped like a geodesic dome. She was conservatively dressed. When she stood, she carried herself with a grace and self-assurance that the young man found instantly attractive. She was tall and probably aging, but one could scarcely tell, given her energy and the sharp glint in her eyes. She motioned for him to sit down.

Her voice was cool water soothing his nerves. "Our mutual friend just called and said you wanted to meet The Inner Manager."

"Well, I...don't know much about him."

She smiled, the lines in her face smoothing into a sculpture of Grecian beauty. "You know him infinitely better than you know yourself."

The young man pinched his face in concentration.

She held up her hands, laughing. "I'm not trying to confuse you. I think you'll see that soon enough. But first, I want you to do something very special. Will you try?"

The young man nodded, impressed by the powerful sense of warmth that exuded from the woman. "Excellent," she said. "I want you to set a goal for yourself today. Goals are very important, and you must get in the habit of setting goals for yourself every morning. Or, you can decide on your goals the night before. The following evening, review your goals for the day, to see if you have met them. You might try reviewing the day's events in *reverse order*, looking objectively at everything you said and did that day, deciding which parts need correcting, and reinforcing yourself for the parts done well. Okay?" The young man could only nod his assent. "Very good. Your goal for today will be to listen carefully to everything you hear, and try to reserve your judgement until later. Fair enough?"

He couldn't resist her charm. He returned her warm smile, amazed at how good it made him feel. "Fair enough."

Her eyes seemed to penetrate him. Her face came alive with a golden warmth as she made a decision. "Excellent. I see why our friend recommended you. Now...you must start at the beginning. I want you to meet each of our seven managers. Each runs a separate floor in this building. You'll return to the first floor and start there. After you've interviewed with each manager, I'll see you again."

Dazzled, the young man asked, "Will I meet The Inner Manager as well?"

"I hope so." She smiled so beautifully he could only shuffle from the room.

Standing outside the executive's office, a sudden thought hit the young man. He pulled a small notebook from his coat pocket and wrote quickly, deciding to take careful notes and to study them every day for a month:

<u>NOTES</u>

1. Make goals for yourself every day, and review your goals that night. Reinforce yourself for things done well, and correct whatever needs to be changed.

2. Listen carefully to other people and reserve judgement. Keep an open mind.

3. Work hard at changing yourself, trying to be objective about your faults and merits.

TRY

TRY

TRY

TRY

HARDER

PRISM OF SELF

The young man rode the elevator to the first floor and entered the reception area. To his surprise, a portly man was waiting for him. The executive stuck out his hand and greeted him warmly. Raw force exuded from the broad palm. "Welcome," he said. "It is a great pleasure to meet you. I'm the Director of Advertising."

Dazed by the man's energy, the visitor could only mumble his salutations and follow the dynamic fellow into his office. The room was colorful and expansive, with a number of prisms and glass structures decorating the windows and furniture. The man indicated a chair. The neophyte took it, trying to relax.

The director leaned forward on the edge of his desk. "Our friend upstairs tells me you'd like to meet The Inner Manager."

Sheepish, the young man said, "Yes, but...I'm a bit confused as to who he..."

"No matter," the administrator boomed. "You'll understand soon enough. First, I'd like to ask you a question. Take a look at this prism." He picked up a glass pyramid and held it to the window, allowing light to strike the surface. Tiers of rainbows were produced on the opposite wall. "What do you see?"

"Colors. Patterns."

"Ah, but what else?"

"I...don't understand."

"Think! Look closely."

He studied the shifting patterns of light. Reflecting, it suddenly struck the young man. "I can see whatever I want."

"Excellent! Our friend said you were a good student. Now, what do you suppose this pyramid represents, in a greater sense?"

"Represents? Well...it changes the rays of light and projects them on the wall, but..."

The director shifted his position. "Yes, but stop and think. If we see whatever we want, what does that tell you about the human mind?"

"That we're good at confusing ourselves?"

"Bravo!" the large man boomed, clapping his hands. "In fact, we often have difficulty telling illusion from reality. It is only through the consensus of others that we decide what is real and what isn't."

"Doesn't that put us in a rather precarious position? I mean, what if others are wrong, but we accept their opinions as fact?"

The executive looked as though he would burst from excitement. "You've got it! You can imagine the massive communication problems between people, when even small things become so muddled. For example, if you look at a line head-on, from one direction only, it looks like a dot. But is it really just a dot? And if you look at a two-dimensional plane from the side, it looks like a line. But is it a line? You see?"

"From which direction?" asked the young man. The two laughed, their mirth jostling the prisms hanging by the window. "You mean everything is relative, as Einstein said. But what does that have to do with the pyramid?"

The mentor beamed. "Only everything. We know that time and even physical space are relative. That means time and space change, as a function of one's point of view. We assume physical reality is concrete and solid, but we forget that matter is made of energy, and energy changes constantly. But it often happens more slowly than our senses can register."

"That's fascinating."

"Yes, it is. Now, suppose Einstein was referring to more than the physical world with his theory of relativity. That is...what if the mind is also an energy field, more than just the physical brain? Would that suggest the mind interacts with the physical world?"

The young man was stunned. "Are you saying..."

The executive hurried on. "Never mind, I'm getting ahead of myself. For now, let's focus on the parallels between the prism and the mind. The prism splits light into its component frequencies, just as the mind splits information into different channels. The difference is that the mind further reassembles the information into patterns of *perception*."

The young man couldn't restrain himself. "If the splitting or rechanneling is biased, the patterns of perception might not correspond to the external world, or to anyone else's ideas about *reality*."

The older man was exuberant. "How quick you are! When one's perceptions are out of synchrony with another's, communication misses. To avoid this, you must keep an open mind at all times, and keep collecting information. Constantly revise your perceptions and theories in a flexible, ever-changing manner, like the ever-changing patterns of light from the prism. Never assume you know everything, no matter how wise or knowledgeable you become - for you are but a fool compared to all there is."

Inundated with thought, the visitor could barely find his tongue. "Of that I'm sure, but...what does that have to do with running a business, or with advertising?"

His host gave a mock scowl. He drew up his shoulders and spoke with conviction. "Once again, only everything. To run a business, one must constantly keep abreast of everything around him. He must use his senses and intuition, his mind and his energy to continuously adjust to a changing world. Emotional fixations and pet beliefs must never enslave the mind."

"You mean there's more to this than meets the mind?"

The executive laughed. "Or more to the mind than meets the brain. And as for advertising...since perception is so variable, it can be created in your audience. Emotions can be aroused, then attached via false beliefs to the products or ideas to be sold. For example, sexual interest is often excited, then attached to products which have nothing to do with sex or sex appeal. I mean, just how sexy is grapefruit juice?"

"I see what you mean. But isn't it done all the time, and successfully?"

The mentor's brows darkened. "Yes, but be warned. Ideally, your advertising must exude positive energy, and make people feel good about themselves and the product. As long as it is a good product and the advertising is fair and honest, all is well. But to falsely represent a product or service is to bring eventual repercussions upon yourself which few people today understand."

"Repercussions?"

"It is like Newton's Third Law of Motion - for every action, there is an equal and opposite reaction. This applies to people and to businesses, as well as to the forces of physics. Violaters of this law must learn the hard way, so that others might learn from their folly."

"It applies to people too? You mean like *karma*, and *you reap what you sow?*"

The director beamed with energy. "The law has been expressed in many forms, my friend. Emotion is energy, and is shaped, focused and directed by thought. As energy, it follows the laws of energy. Therefore, if you advertise an illusion and sell it, you will eventually lose what you cost others. But if you sell a great product which helps others tremendously, you will reap a corresponding reward. It's that simple, and that hard to believe."

"You mean...*what goes around comes around. You get what you pay for. You...*"

The executive laughed and shook his hand. "You have the idea, my friend."

The visitor thanked the man profusely as he was led from the room. Immensely excited, he couldn't wait to meet The Inner Manager.

Before the elevator arrived, the young man extracted his notebook and jotted furiously, determined to read over the notes at least once a day for the next month:

<u>NOTES</u>

1. All perception is relative.

*2. Our cherished **realities** are often illusions, made of fixated emotions and false beliefs.*

3. Keep an open mind, and revise your opinions and perceptions with each new piece of information.

4. For every action there is an equal and opposite reaction - even in the worlds of emotion and business.

5. Emotion is energy, shaped and directed by thought.

THE MIRROR WITHIN

Filled with energy, the young man boarded the elevator and punched the button for the second floor. New ideas were playing at his mind, inundating him with a sense of excitement and joy.

As he stared at the indicator light, the back of his neck began to prickle. He suddenly felt the presence of someone behind him. He abruptly turned and looked into the sweet hazel eyes of a beautiful woman with brilliant blond hair. He felt like a deer caught in the headlights of a car. He wanted to move, but his muscles wouldn't respond. He could only look at her.

She was of medium height and dressed in dark colors that offset her striking hair. She smiled at him, and he thought his heart would implode. When he could breathe again, he remembered he was happily married. He felt guilty over his powerful attraction for this woman.

Irradiant, she seemed to understand. When she spoke, her soft tones paralyzed him. "I believe you're on your way to meet me. I'm the Director of Sales."

The young man could only nod and feign consciousness. How could he have failed to notice her when he entered the elevator? And how did she know who he was...or where he was going?

The doors opened on the second floor, and she gestured for him to lead the way. She flowed along beside him, a stream of light on legs. They walked into her office, which was decorated with plush furniture, warm carpeting and modern art. They sat opposite one another in comfortable swivel chairs.

He finally found his voice. "It's a pleasure to meet you. You know, everyone here just... glows."

Her smile was enigmatic, reminding him of the Mona Lisa. "Well, not all the time. We have our problems, but we've found that cultivating the right attitudes about life and business makes people happier. That inner satisfaction shows, and causes things to work for you, instead of against you."

"I see," he said, when he really didn't. He tried to take his eyes off her, but it was futile.

"In fact," the executive continued, "how much one loves and respects oneself is the key to how one relates to others. And, it is the key to sales. If a person maintains a magnetically positive self-image, it communicates to others in a positive way. It makes others feel good, and they enjoy being around the positive person. Such a person can walk into a room and instantly light it up. It's been called magnetism, charisma, and a host of other names, but the principle is always the same."

The young man nodded, fascinated by this vibrant woman. "You mean others see a happy person, and it makes them want to be happy too."

She smiled, the blond hair a halo about her face. "Well, that's part of it. But we've also found that energy actually transfers from one person to another, like electricity and magnetism."

"Literally? You mean like...radiation?"

Her eyes grew wider, her pupils black holes of infinite attraction. "Yes. You've felt positive energy radiating between people here - that's the energy of pure love. Now negative energy, that has a very different effect on people. Can you guess what it is?"

"Well, I've known some very negative people."

"How did they make you feel?"

"I guess the way my stomach feels now."

"Like squirming larvae trying to mutate into divine butterflies?"

He grinned. "How did you know?"

Her eyes were brilliant stars. "That's the way most people feel when they confront the unknown. And it's the way people feel when they're upset by a negative personality. Since you're confronting many new ideas today, I'll assume that's the cause of your momentary distress, and not the present company." She laughed gaily.

"No, no," he protested, waving his hands. Her humor was infectious, and he joined in her laughter. He finally began to relax.

"That's great," she said. "If we're positive personalities, then we attract others who are positive, and repel those who are negative. But if we're negative personalities, then we attract others who are negative, and repel those who are positive."

He shook his head firmly. "But...that reduces people to being no more than magnets, attracting and repelling in the matrices of ambulant night!"

Her laughter was silver rain. "Our friends didn't tell me you were poetic!"

Sheepishly, he said, "I'm usually not."

Her eyes enveloped him in energy. "Many more things will change." She hurried on. "We are infinitely more than magnets, but our social connections tend to be regulated by what we're feeling at the time we meet others. By being aware of the process, we gain control over it."

"It sounds too simple."

"Most truths are. Complexity often arises from confusion, not from a greater intellect, as many would presume."

He was stunned. She continued, "Remember what the Director of Advertising told you? People reap what they sow. It acts like a boomerang - what you give off comes back to you. If you project positive thoughts and feelings, you attract positive people and life circumstances. The same applies to the negative. You see?"

He shifted uneasily in his chair. "Logically, how does that make sense?"

"Logically? What is logic, but the end result of arbitrary assumptions? And if your assumptions are wrong, your conclusions will be equally wrong. For example, if you insist that the material world is all there is, because that's all you can see with your eyes, then you will be enslaved by your senses, unable to see beyond the murky veil of matter."

"Is that an assumption...or presumption?"

Her smile was a luminous kiss. "To assume that the limits of the universe are bounded by man's physical senses is the worst form of presumption. And remember...*the level of one's arrogance occurs in direct proportion to the level of one's ignorance.*"

The young man clapped his hands. "I'm going to remember that comment."

"Many have tunnel vision, but fail to realize it. The world has temporarily become a place of dark materialism, where matter is worshipped as God. Despite our technological advances, this is the darkest of ages."

The visitor was stunned. "Matter as God? The darkest of ages?"

Her eyes became prophetic. "It seems paradoxical, doesn't it? We've put men on the moon, but we've lost our way. We can destroy the world, but can we build a better one? We've become so buried in the fruitless pursuit of lower passions that we believe the higher ones no longer exist. The only consolation is that these negative conditions will not last, because negativity tends to destroy itself." She smiled ruefully. "Of course, we do have to help it along at times."

Hesitantly, he asked, "What can we do to change it?"

"We must each follow a higher code of *responsibility* in our behavior. If we do otherwise, we sow the seeds of our discontent. Everything we do comes back on us, so we must do what is right for others, as well as for ourselves."

"Do unto others?"

She nodded, the golden radiance beaming. "How we see others and how we treat them is a projection of how we see ourselves. If we dislike others, then we must work on changing ourselves, for that is where the problem begins. The great mistake of many reformers through history has been to try to change the world. Because of free will, no one can force another person to change. Each person must change oneself, or pay the consequences."

He smiled cynically. "Tell that to the corporate state that rules the world, the shadow government behind all governments."

Her brows knitted. "I see you've learned much of importance about this world. All I can tell you is that chickens always come home to roost."

He pondered this. "So *those who try to enslave the world are actually enslaved themselves...by their lower passions!*"

"Precisely! We tend to attract whatever we desire or fear in life. Remember *the self-fulfilling prophecy*...we tend to make happen either what we expect to happen, or what we fear will happen. If a person is paranoid about being controlled, he will perform paranoid control trips on others."

The young man was getting excited. "That's why many people believe they're always right, because we see what we project!"

Her blithe radiance bloomed. "Yes. We see the world through our own self-image. If that self-image is negative, we attract negative people and circumstances to us, convinced it is reality, and not the shadowy contours of our own creations reflecting back to us. That type of illusion-making is at the root of many ills."

He felt a trifle frightened, wondering how his own negative thoughts and feelings had long affected his life without his realizing it. "That's why we can't blindly believe our senses, without understanding the process behind it!"

"Bravo!" she cried. She looked as though she wanted to hug him.

He raced on. "How does the negative self-image form in the first place?"

She said gently, "Think back to your own childhood and all the times you were scolded unfairly or insulted by overbearing adults. Remember the times other children stomped on your ego with their cruelty and stupidity. Perhaps you held your emotions inside, allowing them to stew and build, only to come out in another form at a later time. Perhaps you blamed or attacked someone else, without realizing what you were doing."

The young man felt ashamed.

She nodded. "Don't beat yourself up anymore for it. Forgive yourself, and forgive all who have harmed you. But most important, learn from your lessons never to repeat those negative behaviors again. To assist this process, you must be aware of any negative thoughts as soon as they come up, and instantly replace them with positive thoughts about yourself and others. This has the effect of programming the mind to work in a positive way at all times. Find something positive in all things, and it will be returned to you many times over."

"That's all there is to it?"

"Hardly, but it's a beginning. And it's more difficult than it sounds. But with time, as these practices become habits, you begin to acquire a powerfully positive self-image. This lets you turn your desires into realities, rather than turning your fears into realities, as negative thinking will do. You see?"

The young man felt overwhelmed. "You mean you have to monitor your thoughts and feelings all the time?"

She shook her head. "Only when they stray into the negative, when you must instantly replace them with positive ones. This is most important, and is a great secret to successful sales and to a successful life. Can you do it?"

He shrugged with feigned confidence. "If it's that important..."

She smiled. "It's that, and more. Now, I believe our friend upstairs is waiting for you."

As he waited for the elevator, the young man wrote in his notebook, again determined to study the notes at least once a day for a month:

<u>NOTES</u>

1. Think positive thoughts at all times, to attract positive people and positive life circumstances.

2. Thinking negative attracts negative people and negative life circumstances.

3. The best business deal equally benefits all parties involved. This produces positive effects for all.

*4. We create what we expect to happen or what we fear will happen, and then perceive our creations as if they were physical reality all along. Convinced that our senses couldn't lie to us, we often fail to see the process behind perception. **A belief in objectivity is therefore totally subjective.***

5. We must replace negative thoughts and feelings with positive ones and find the good in all things, in order to make our desires into realities. Otherwise, we will blindly make our fears into realities.

YOU ARE

WHAT

YOU *FEEL*

POLISHING THE MIRROR

The young man boarded the elevator once more, his mind alive with ideas, his heart beating at a faster pace. The elevator jolted to a stop on the third floor and the doors opened. He stepped out and met a short, energetic man who repeatedly pumped his arm.

"It is a great pleasure to meet you," the little man boomed, his voice filling the corridor. He escorted the visitor into his office. "Sit down, please."

The student took a comfortable chair and surveyed the suite. The pine tables were sprinkled with futuristic devices that were either new inventions or science fiction memorabilia.

"I am the Director of Human Resources, my friend. Do you know what those are?"

The visitor thought for a moment. "Earlier today I might have said yes to that question, but now, I think I'd better hold my tongue."

The little man laughed, his wizened face breaking into a thousand lines of mirth. "That is a sage answer. You're learning fast." His dark, bushy brows knotted as his expression changed.

"I trust other secrets of human resources will soon become clear to you. How is your energy holding up?"

The young man grinned. "Considering the rate of influx...reasonably well."

"Good." The brows almost kissed. His voice bubbled with energy. "Now, I believe you've learned the importance of distinguishing illusion from reality, and the necessity of developing a positive self-image. Next, we need to learn how to program the subconscious mind. That is the greatest human resource of all. Does that sound interesting?"

"Yes!"

"Great! As you know, building a positive self-image is profoundly important. How do you suppose this process works?" His eyes became pinpoints of brown force, boring into the young man.

The neophyte shifted uneasily in his chair. "I guess if you believe in yourself enough, it starts to come true."

The director almost bounded from his chair. His energy seemed infinite. "Excellent! But what makes that process work?"

"I couldn't begin to tell you."

"Oh, I don't know. You might begin, but not know where to end." The executive stood abruptly and paced the room. "Think of consciousness as having many levels to it, much like the concentric layers about an onion. Most people get stuck at one of those levels, without realizing so many more exist. It's like living inside a house all your life, and never stepping outside!"

"I see."

"I'm sure you do. That's why you're here."

"I beg your..."

"Pardon? All in good time. All in good time. But why do people get stuck?"

The young man pondered. "Bad habits?"

"Exactly! We become hypnotized into certain frequencies or patterns of thought by our emotional fixations. Conversely, our emotions are held in frozen, cyclic currents by our beliefs and attitudes. It works both ways. Thoughts focus and shape our emotions, while our emotions color and bias our thoughts."

"Why can't we tell what's happening?"

"Thanks to the self-fulfilling prophecy, what we expect to happen is what we make happen. And no matter what we make happen, we are soon convinced we were right all along!"

"But...hypnotized? Isn't that a bit strong?"

The administrator shot his finger into the air. "Not at all! We hypnotize ourselves into believing certain things with the internal statements we repeat time and again. Things like...I'm no good, I'm a failure, and so on. These statements become habits and we soon believe them, no matter how irrational they might be."

"You mean we lie to ourselves and don't know it?"

"Yes, but we don't mean to lie. We just don't see the process for what it is. And the more rigid our fixated emotions, the more we cling to our irrational beliefs, insisting we are right when we are truly seeing our own projections reflected off a given situation."

The young man sat on the edge of his chair. "That explains why different people see things so differently, yet each is certain that he or she is right."

The instructor seemed to grow more excited by the minute. "Precisely. Now, suppose you have a profoundly positive self-image. The very center of your mind will exude positive energy, because the self-image is at the center of the mind! That positive energy flows through all the layers of the mind and beyond, to affect other people. You can think of the mind as a television broadcasting station, where the frequency broadcast is determined by the emotions flowing within, and the events in the broadcast are determined by the thoughts held in mind during the emotionalized broadcast."

The young man fixed his concentration on the executive. "Now I know you're joking."

"Not at all. Einstein proved that all matter is energy, temporarily stabilized into a specific form. The forms change with time, as a function of other energy fields acting upon them. The human brain is one such material form, and a very complex one, but it is surrounded and subfused by an even more complex energy field, which we call the mind. The mind gives off energy at a wavelength determined by the emotions, and projected into a form determined by the guiding power of thought."

Anxiety flushed through the young man. He wanted to bolt from the room. "Now, wait a minute...I came here to learn about business."

"Relax, my friend. There is nothing to fear. You are simply encountering the unknown, and it is always frightening at first. Soon, it will all make sense."

The young man started to stand. "I don't know, I..."

The executive spoke in a soothing voice. "You can prove it to yourself. Just relax, and start breathing long, deep breaths. Then, you can tense and relax all the major muscle groups of the body. You will be instructed in that later today. Next, feed whatever desire you wish to create into the subconscious mind - which is misnamed, because it is really the *superconscious mind* within! Concentrate on the idea intensely, lucidly visualizing it with all your senses. You must see, taste, hear, feel and smell what you want to come true, holding no other thoughts in mind while you visualize. Power the visualization with intense emotional energy, get excited about it!"

"Then what? I push a button and my wish is my command?"

"Hardly." The executive became stern. "After you have visualized the desired result, you must let it go. Forget about it for the moment, and assume it will come true. Then, do everything in your power physically to make it come true. Work hard toward that objective, and never doubt for a moment that you will achieve the desired result. Perform the visualization exercise several times a day. More difficult and complex objectives take more time and more intense visualizations. And you must be careful not to contradict the desired result with conflicting thoughts and feelings, such as doubt, or you might sabotage the objective."

The young man was beyond words. "You're ...serious, aren't you? You make it sound so...scientific."

The director beamed. "That is precisely what it is. The new field of *biomagnetics* has to do with studying energy dynamics around and within living organisms. The field is embryonic, and much will be discovered in the future. But you must be cautioned in using any of these techniques, for each of them carries a very heavy price. You must remember that everything you do in this world comes back on you. If you do anything that will be destructive to yourself or others, you will pay for every ounce of pain and suffering caused."

The visitor scrutinized a thought. *"The world is a mirror, as is the inner self. The world reflects you and you reflect the world."*

"Excellent!" The executive seemed to be amazed. "You must therefore direct the superconscious mind to only create results which will bring good to yourself and all others involved."

The student sat in concentration for some time. "We must therefore create *win-win* situations, where everybody benefits. Cooperative competition, you might say."

"Wonderful!" The director smiled. "You do learn fast, my friend. The best business deal is where everyone wins, establishing positive relations for future deals."

Overwhelmed but excited, the neophyte had a faraway look in his eyes. "It's so incredible."

"There's another important point before I let you go. In order to broadcast successful results on a more continuous basis, you must transform all your lower emotions into higher ones. Cleansing the field of pollutants, you might say. Only then can you transcend the interference of lower frequencies unintentionally broadcast at the same time, masking and confusing your desires."

"Lower emotions?"

"Fear. Anxiety. Guilt. Depression. All the learned negative reactions we acquire, reactions toward other people and events in our lives. These reactions greatly hamper us and sabotage our more positive efforts."

The young man was mesmerized. "You know, I've felt that before."

"Good. Tune into your feelings and thoughts. Be aware of what you're thinking and feeling, and how you affect others. We must each take responsibility for how we influence others, since we will pay for the consequences of those acts. Above all, you must learn to love others no matter how they treat you, for this frees you of the entangling fixations of negative emotion. This doesn't mean you can't fight back, but it does mean to stand clear of the emotional carnage that lies there."

The student could only nod his assent. The fear of moments before had subsided, now replaced by a feeling of enchantment. He allowed himself to be led from the room.

The tiny but powerful man waved goodbye as the visitor stood by the elevator. The young man took many long, deep breaths, wondering what wonders lay ahead.

Riding the elevator, the young man took out his notebook and wrote furiously, the ideas flooding his mind. As before, he decided to study the notes at least once a day for a month:

<u>NOTES</u>

1. The mind has many levels, like an onion. Emotions can freeze thoughts and attitudes at a given level, just as thoughts give shape and direction to emotions.

2. To create what you desire, relax the mind and body, then focus the mind on the results you want. Get excited about the idea, creating vivid images using all the senses. Then release the images and forget about it, until the next visualization. Do everything in your power physically to make it come true.

3. Make certain that all goals desired will obtain the greatest good for the greatest number of people involved. Assume responsibility for every thought, emotion and behavior you create, for you will pay for each.

*4. Observe your emotional responses to situations as they arise, noting which thoughts attach to which emotions. **Whenever negative thoughts or emotions appear, replace them immediately with positive ones.***

5. Love others no matter how they treat you, for this frees the heart and mind from the bonding illusions of negative emotion.

CONCENTRATION

The young man exited the elevator on the fourth floor. His apprehension mellowing, a sense of calm descended over him. The office door in front of him opened, revealing a rotund woman. She was elegantly dressed, her hair blown back, as if from the wind. She put her hands on her hips and smiled. When she spoke, her voice was fluted like a bird's.

"Welcome," she trilled, offering her hand. A trifle uncomfortable, he took it. She waved him into the office. He was startled by the contrast with the other offices he had seen. A profusion of books, charts and graphs covered the floor and dusty furniture.

Following his gaze, she laughed. "I hope you don't mind the mess. I don't get many visitors. Most of my work is in research, so I usually fraternize with books, computers and graphs. But do come in, please."

He followed her lead and sat in a dilapidated chair, after removing a pile of books and debris. "Thank you," he said, slowly warming to her smile.

She sat behind her desk and pushed aside a stack of texts to get a better look at him. "I suppose I should introduce myself. I'm the Director of Manufacturing." She waved down his surprise. "I mostly research new manufacturing techniques, searching for new and better ways to produce things. It's a journey that never ends."

He returned her infectious laugh. "It's a pleasure to meet you."

She bowed gently, mirth playing about her lips. "By now I suppose you've heard all about the self-image, programming the superconscious mind, and how to tell an Einsteinian ring from a Newtonian apple, right?"

"That and a few other things."

"Excellent. Now we must elaborate a bit more. In order to program the superconscious mind, we must learn to properly concentrate and visualize our thoughts. The right combination of factors must be brought together to make it all work. In a sense, that's the basis of manufacturing. Put together the right materials in the right way, with an ounce of ingenuity, and you've got a mansion or a skyscraper." Her eyes sparkled beneath her graying black hair.

"That makes sense."

"And more. But before you can properly visualize, you must learn to totally relax and clear your mind of interfering thoughts and feelings. Life is full of tensions and anxieties, which you must learn to subordinate to your will and your mind. You must not allow the negativities thrown at you by others, such as rude drivers and arrogant salespeople, to displace your inner peace. To assist this process, make it a habit to breathe long, deep breaths throughout the day. Breathe in slowly through your nostrils, hold for a few seconds, then exhale through your nostrils."

The young man smiled. "This sounds like yoga."

She seemed to radiate peace. "Used by many disciplines, one cannot overemphasize the importance of proper breathing. Before you retire at night, and in the morning, make a habit of tensing and relaxing all the major muscle groups of the body. First, breathe long, deep breaths, then tense your forearms and wrists for ten seconds at three-quarters strength. Then relax, focus on how different it feels, while breathing the deep breaths. Then similarly tense and relax the upper arms; shoulders and neck; chest, stomach and back muscles; then the thigh and calf muscles. Throughout this procedure, keep clearing the mind of all interfering thoughts."

"Wipe clean the mental screen, focusing only on your breathing and how good it feels to relax. Once the entire body is relaxed, you are ready to begin the visualization."

As he listened, the young man began breathing long, deep breaths. The woman smiled. "Good! That's the idea. You can use part of the relaxation procedure while at work or with friends, where you tense and relax just one or two muscle groups. The only time you should not use this procedure is while driving a car or using any other type of motor vehicle or potentially dangerous equipment! This is most important."

The young man nodded, entranced by her melodic words. She continued, "The next step is to create a clear and vivid image of what you want to create. See it sharply in the mind's eye, imagining all the aspects of the goal you wish to reach. See it in full color, painting in all the details of the scene. Let your images have vivid proportions, which move and cast shadows. Let them smell and taste and feel. Hold the visualization for several minutes if possible, brushing aside all distracting thoughts and feelings. Get excited about it, want it to happen. Then release it and forget about it for the time being, assuming it will happen. Repeat this procedure a few times each day for as long as it takes to make it come true, and do everything in your power physically to make it happen. Never doubt the power of your thoughts and feelings! If you doubt the results in any way, you will sabotage your own efforts."

The young man was deep in thought. "I suppose most of us doubt such things are possible from the start, defeating the process before it begins."

"Exactly! None of us are born losers. We learn to lose, just as we must learn to win."

"The self-fulfilling prophecy..."

"Is often less than fulfilling. But it teaches us great things, if we open our minds."

The young man was in awe. "It sounds so simple. Why is it so hard to see?"

"We see what we project, and we project what we feel. Learn to feel and project love, pure love, and your mind will clear for the first time in your life. If you feel and project lower emotions, such as anger, anxiety, depression, guilt, envy and so on, then that is all you will see. And it is all you will attract from others."

The neophyte became rueful. "I can see I have much to learn."

Her smile seemed to inundate the room. "So do we all, and it never ends. One more point - you can learn to visualize more sharply by closely observing the world around you. Study the contours and shadows of everything you see, noting the precise colors and their variations, the relative sizes and shapes of things, the different effects of light on objects. Study the world the way an artist would, then recreate it later in your mind. Try to visualize the images as clearly as you can, with your eyes closed. As you observe more closely, so will you recreate."

He closed his eyes for a moment, then opened one and looked at her. "I think I see what you..."

They both laughed as she stood and escorted him to the door. "You are learning fast, my friend. *May you know peace* as you begin the upward journey."

As she closed the door he took a mental snapshot of her, focusing on the sparkling eyes beneath the shock of incongruent hair.

Pausing in the corridor, he scribbled in his notebook, again with the determination to study the notes at least once a day for a month:

NOTES

1. Stay relaxed throughout the day, and focus on inner peace. Love others no matter how they treat you, for this frees the mind from the bondage of lower emotions.

2. Concentration means seeing an image in the mind to the exclusion of all else, making it come alive with the senses and the emotions.

3. To visualize more clearly and accurately, observe the world closely, noting its details, colors and patterns.

4. Create an image in the mind of what you want to accomplish, seeing it in detail, with its colors, patterns, shadows and sensual dimensions. Hold the image as long as you can, then release it, assume it will come true, and do everything you can physically to make it happen. Repeat as needed.

<u>*BEWARE*</u>

YOUR *DESIRES*

AND

FEARS...

FOR YOU *WILL*

CREATE THEM !

INTEGRATION

The young man found his way to the fifth floor. He was becoming weary from the mental exertion, but a strange sense of strength seemed to burn within him. He knew he had to keep going. He walked to the office door facing the elevator and knocked.

The door burst open. A towering man with broad shoulders filled the frame. Brown hair and blue eyes offset the rugged face. The cleft chin accented the pursed lips. He stuck out a powerful hand and pumped the visitor into the room.

"Welcome, my friend. Welcome indeed. I have heard much about you. You are becoming a renowned student here. Perhaps some day you can...well, that's for a later time. Do come in and sit down. Would you like some tea? Coffee?"

The visitor was overwhelmed by the herculean fellow. With some effort he found his voice. "Tea, thank you."

"Great!" The giant walked to a small table and poured hot water into cups, then dropped in tea bags. "Cream? Sugar? Honey?"

"Honey, please."

The man brought the steaming cups, then sat opposite the neophyte in a straight-backed chair. The young man surveyed the room, impressed by the blend of modern and antique furniture. An array of computer equipment banked the far wall, reminding the visitor of a spaceship console.

"Perhaps I should introduce myself," the giant boomed. "I'm the Director of Artificial Intelligence. Which is not to say I'm a politician."

They both laughed. The director continued. "We're the leading edge around here, when it comes to gadgetry and technological interventions. But we claim no supremacy over our neighbor departments in other respects."

They again laughed. The young man almost commented on that point, given the director's size, but he restrained himself.

The instructor leaned forward, as if consumed by a conspiratorial sense. He laced his thick fingers together, his eyes boring into the young man. "Now...the basic functions of the intellectual part of the mind are similar to the basic functions of a computer. Did you know that? No? Ah. Let's start with memory. Both the computer and the mind would be lost without memory. If information isn't stored properly, it can't be recalled for later use, such as for contrasting and comparing different bits of information, for use as part of logical deduction and induction, and for use in creating new ideas and products."

The visitor smiled. "Daily life would be impossible...as it is for patients with Alzheimer's disease."

"Precisely." The director used his hands when he spoke, bringing them together and drawing them apart as if opposing magnets controlled their motion. "Memory gives the mind nominal functions, where it assigns names and identities to external objects for future reference. This is most important in coordinating oneself around the physical world."

The visitor nodded, excited by the ideas. The executive continued. "Next, the mind has ordinal functions, where it assigns ranks, or values to the objects internally represented. This is one place where emotion comes into play. Things liked or desired are given positive values, while things disliked or feared are given negative values."

The young man was becoming exuberant. "It's all so mathematical, like...a new physics of the mind!"

The giant radiated warmth. "You do learn fast. This is indeed the new physics, part of the unified field theory Einstein searched for his entire life. The part of the equation that Einstein omitted was...the mind."

The visitor's eyes were lighting up. "The creative power of mind...biasing our frames of reference, creating our personal worlds around us...which reflect back to us the nature of what we've created. Incredible! Maybe this crazy world makes sense, after all!"

"And then some. But to continue...we create positive and negative charges in the mind by what we like and dislike, derived from our experiences and stored by memory. This creates a charged field. Some parts of the field are positive, some are negative, and some are neutral. Similar to the atmosphere about the earth, the different charges clash. This causes vortices and spinning storms of conflicting emotions, which cloud thought and confuse one's actions. These emotional storms can be set off by any number of events, such as stress, conflicts with another person's value system, and so on."

The visitor could hardly contain himself. "So our habits of thought and feeling keep these storms raging and get us into trouble time and again...until we change the system."

The administrator smiled his approval. "You've got it. And remember that the values we give our internal symbols are completely arbitrary, and might have nothing to do with the actual values of the things represented in the external world."

"So...our internal reconstructions of the external world, and the actual external world could be vastly different. That *would* cause confusion!"

The large man nodded, his hands weaving patterns in the air. "That is the basis of many psychological problems. If you misperceive the external world, including the actions and motives of other people, you can imagine the difficulties you create for yourself."

The young man was ecstatic, overwhelmed by the ideas. The air seemed to crackle with energy. "Psychology becomes more of a science, when viewed from that perspective."

The elder grinned. "That's it again! Instead of using statistics to estimate behavior based on probabilities and other inaccurate methods, we will one day be able to make images of the energy fields about the mind. Then man might know himself..."

"I can't wait! Can you imagine..."

"And then some. But first, I must finish explaining...once the mind has created ordinal values by rank ordering its images, it can then compare and contrast one thing to another. For example, we decide which toy we like best as children, and which friend we like best as soon as we know what a friend means. And then we learn more complex symbols. We learn an alphabet so we can communicate oral and written speech to each other, and we learn to count by numbers so we can keep track of how many things we have."

The visitor jumped in. "We compare numbers to see which is larger, and later do more complex operations like addition, subtraction, multiplication and division. This involves the critical, or analytical processes of the mind."

The executive looked at him sideways. "You sure you haven't been here before?" They both laughed. "In any case, besides the analytical functions, the mind also has creative processes. We use the imagination to expand, contract, reverse or otherwise distort our mental images, producing any form of fantasy we desire or fear."

The neophyte rose out of his chair, carried away by the ideas. He paced the room. "So the analytical processes break down things and look at them critically, to understand their meaning and worth, and the creative processes put them back together into new forms."

The giant stood up and shook his hand. "Exactly. The mind can then create cause-effect sequences which attempt to explain why the physical world works the way it does, and why the social world works the way it does. We call these sequences *schemes*, or tapes, which are really belief systems about the nature of physical or social reality."

"And if we attach strong emotions to those tapes, we play them over and over, convincing ourselves they're right, even when they're not."

The administrator nodded. "If we allow our emotions to bond with certain thoughts, thoughts which we choose to believe because we either desire or fear what they represent, then yes, that is precisely what happens. We see what we want to see, and proceed to make it come true using the creative power of mind."

The young man whistled. He stood by a window, looking through the silver pane at the expanse of the city. He turned to the instructor. "Perhaps we have both analytical and creative functions so we can better understand what we've created..."

The executive smiled a cryptic smile, his face strangely aglow. He didn't answer. The young man continued. "How can we develop our mental functions, to further advance ourselves?"

The director blinked several times, searching for the right words. "There are many ways. First, you must learn to relax, concentrate and visualize. You must get proper sleep, diet, and exercise, and learn to think positively at all times. You must learn to convert all your negative feelings into positive ones...you will learn more about that later."

"But..."

"For now, think about this. The brain has two hemispheres, right and left. For most people, the right hemisphere intakes new information before it becomes linked to verbal functions and stored in the left hemisphere. The left hemisphere is usually the center of verbal activities, and the right handles more visual-spatial information, as well as incoming information. These are generalizations, but it helps us in our creative thinking. For example, it expands your creative thinking to combine verbal with visual activities."

"Verbal with visual? You mean like hearing what you see and seeing what you hear?"

The executive laughed. "Something like that. But I was thinking more about doing things that get both hemispheres working together and interacting."

"Dueling hemispheres, you might say?"

The director laughed again, his hands catching an invisible ball of magnetism. "Yes. And the mind is developed by practicing activities that stimulate its many functions. For example, working crossword puzzles stimulates verbal functions, and playing chess stimulates spatial functions. Combining verbal and spatial functions is especially rewarding. Suppose you've had trouble in the past remembering people's names. If you meet someone by the name of Bill, and he has a big nose, you might better remember his name by visualizing that large nose rising from his face, like a bill on a bird. You see?"

"It's easy! If someone's name is George and he has a cleft chin, you might think of that cleft as a gorge, reminding you of the name George."

"That's it. You can remember words or names better by associating them with a visual picture."

"Incredible. But how does all this fit together into the big picture?"

The executive paused, his lips pursed. "After the mind has learned to use its powers of naming, ranking and logical thinking, it can build more complex sequences and hierarchies of thought. Interpretations and conjectures about reality are arrived at, which are tested against the outside world to see if they're true."

The young man smiled ironically. "You mean they're tested if the person remains objective. If not, illusions grow."

"Very good. And throughout this process, you can program information to the superconscious mind, to get its feedback and direction in your problem-solving. It is a great resource, when you know how to tap it."

Pondering this, the young man shuffled his rubber soles on the carpet, then inadvertently touched the metal lamp beside him. A spark leapt from his fingers to the lamp, startling him.

"Perfect!" the director bellowed, further startling the visitor. "That is precisely what I was talking about. As the conscious and superconscious minds move closer together, more and more energy sparks between them. This opens the doors for higher creative abilities to leap from the superconscious to the conscious mind. Just as static electricity leapt from your finger to the lamp, so will energy surge from the higher to the lower mind when the conduits are opened."

"Is that all there is to it?"

The elder roared with laughter. "You will do well, for humor is one of the gateways inward. Others are openness of mind and flexibility of thought. Another is humility, for we cannot see beyond the frail but dense vanities of ego. But the most powerful gateways of all are...pure, unselfish love for your fellow human beings, and the supreme desire to do good works upon earth. These are the powers that melt all illusion, and return your conscious focus to the center of the cyclone of mind."

The young man was in another world. He nodded his head appreciatively. As he was escorted to the door, he suspected the identity of The Inner Manager.

Determining to remember the key concepts he had just learned, the young man wrote quickly on his pad:

NOTES

1. Our internal mental images may be different from their external realities.

2. Practicing verbal and spatial exercises stimulates creative thinking.

3. Memory can be improved by combining verbal and spatial information into a single image.

4. The mind has critical and creative functions, which we use to construct our beliefs about reality. If our beliefs and reality do not correspond, psychological problems can result.

5. As the superconscious and conscious minds link, energy and information flows between them. Pathways between the two levels are openness of mind, flexibility of thought, humor, humility and, most important, love.

IMAGINATION

The young man boarded the elevator with a new sense of energy. He felt as though he were entering a larger sphere of thinking, and it was exciting! Most of all, he felt great about himself.

He charged into the hallway on the sixth floor, wondering what marvels awaited him. He knocked on the door of the inner office, and after a moment it opened. A sturdy woman stood before him, her long legs riveted to the floor. Her wavy, black hair undulated in the air, as if charged with electricity. The young man was reminded of a Van de Graaff generator, where a bulb sits on top of a shaft and a positive electrostatic field is generated about the bulb. When he shook her hand, his perceptions were confirmed - the electric charge was there.

"Come in, my friend!" she said happily, her voice several octaves above his. "I've been looking forward to meeting you. This is indeed a pleasure."

He followed her into the room and took an unusally shaped chair - it was a squat pyramid with a seat balanced on the apex. The rest of the furniture in the room was similarly designed, with obelisks and abstract shapes filling the void. He suppressed a whistle as he tried to get comfortable.

She sat opposite him, on a chair composed of three cones with a seat on top of it. "I'm sure you've had quite a day so far. But never fear, there is more to come."

Feeling refreshed despite the time that had passed, he nodded cheerfully. "Absolutely."

"Tremendous. For openers, I'm the Director of Marketing. Here, that's a more unusual position than it would be in most corporations, because of our innovative methods. We have devised a myriad of ways to evolve, promote and distribute our products. Our real work consists of using the imagination. This is a powerful tool, utilizing all the mental functions you've been studying."

"All the functions?" he asked sheepishly.

She smiled gently, her green eyes burning into him. "Yes. You must have a positive self-image as well as a good memory, know how to feed ideas to the superconscious mind, generate love and harmony among others to enlist their help, concentrate and visualize properly, and perform deductive and inductive thinking. Then, combining the above within verbal and spatial patterns, you must bring into contact the conscious and superconscious minds. Can you do all that?"

He thought for a moment. "Maybe not today, but in time..."

"Excellent! It will take time, and it will not be easy. But the rewards are massive, inestimable by most standards." Her voice became fervent, alive with energy. He smiled ruefully - the Van de Graaff generator was pumping.

His excitement showed in his voice. "What exactly is imagination?"

She laughed softly, the Spanish moss hair winging in her energetic winds. "I could say it's the smoke of fires long-tempered by incubation and desire. Or the integration point of all the mind is and does. Or the rearrangement of old ideas broken down into their component parts and forged into new ideas. All of these would be true, but none captures the boundaries of imagination."

The visitor was pensive. "What about the energy dynamics of imagination?"

Her eyes glistened from afar. "The others were right about you, my friend. You are amazing. You might think of imagination as a great vortex of energy, a spinning cyclone in the mind. This cyclone gives birth to holograms, or moving, vibrant images which we create with our thoughts and feelings. Those images are forged from the criss-crossing strains of emotion which we permit ourselves to feel, and the thoughts we allow ourselves to think. In other words, our thoughts and feelings are the channels which tune our minds to any focus we desire or fear."

"So we change mental channels by changing how we think and feel. Incredible!"

"Precisely. And there's more. Our minds are the lenses which burn the holograms into form in the physical world. Those lenses are powered by the strength of our desires or fears behind the visualization. Remember...we are the gatekeepers of our own realities, for our holograms tend to come true in our physical and emotional lives."

A surge of energy flashed through the neophyte as he was struck by an insight. "I'll bet if we set our thoughts and feelings to certain frequencies, we can tune into the superconscious mind and all the wonders it avails us."

He could have sworn that sparks of bluish light orbited her winging hair. No, he thought to himself, it must be my...imagination!

Her eyes penetrated him. "You are referring to intuition, where the superconscious mind can better communicate with the conscious mind when the two are attuned to one another. But remember...the superconscious mind often speaks to you symbolically and in dreams, since what the conscious mind can absorb is limited by one's self-imposed boundaries of belief and expectation."

He nodded slowly. "You mean intuition is like a transducer of energy, a kind of transformer that converts one wavelength to another?"

"Perfect! You are a fast learner. To facilitate those transformations, you must study a wide range of fields, especially in the sciences, the creative arts and psychology. Over time, your mind will make connections in many unexpected directions. Then, as the superconscious and conscious minds come into closer alignment, the imagination will be sparked in countless ways."

He smiled playfully. "I know I'm being premature, but I kind of feel that way now."

Her green eyes were full of mirth. "As you develop your imagination and all the functions which underlie it, you will find your personal force increasing. Your ability to affect other people and the world around you expands, and your sense of well-being develops to a profound degree. Your entire perception of life and the world changes, all for the better."

"That I can believe."

Understanding radiated from her pristine face. "We all undergo dark moments of the soul, trials and tribulations in life. That's how we learn lessons never to be forgotten. Over time, we each develop our own referential field, an internal frame of reference by which we perceive external events and make judgements, interpreting events and deciding on courses of action. And the basic dimensions, or axes of rotation of that internal field are determined by our specific thought-emotion fixation points."

He couldn't restrain himself. "So whatever you think and feel from habit generates your perceptions and the specific experiences of your life. We actually hypnotize ourselves with our feelings and beliefs!"

The green eyes burned brighter. "Once you accept responsibility for this fact and stop trying to blame others or make self-pitying excuses for your actions, you will assume a much greater control over your life."

The visitor glowed with enthusiasm. "And I thought I was coming here to learn about starting my own business!"

Her smile was enigmatic. "Ah, but you are. A properly run business flows from a properly run life. In fact, business and life become synonymous."

As she escorted him to the door, the young man was radiant. "You can't imagine what this has meant to me today."

"Ah, but I can."

Pausing in the hallway, the young man wrote in his notebook, once more resolving to study the notes every day for a month:

NOTES

1. Imagination is the combination and creation of new ideas from the bodies of old ideas.

2. Our sense of reality is created by our fixated feelings and beliefs.

3. We can program our minds with our thoughts and feelings to create in our lives the realities we wish.

4. Imagination combines all our mental functions, to help us dissolve old realities and create new ones.

5. Intuition is the merging of the superconscious and conscious minds.

OUR *THOUGHTS* AND *FEELINGS*

ARE THE *CHANNELS* WHICH

TUNE OUR *MINDS*

TO ANY *FOCUS*

WE *DESIRE* OR *FEAR*

CORPORATE EVOLUTION

Charged with energy, the young man dismissed the elevator and leapt up the stairs, taking three steps at a time. He entered the seventh floor hallway and found the office. He was about to knock when the door opened.

A tall, thin man greeted him with a firm handshake. The man was balding, his pink forehead receding into a lawn of close-cropped hair. The forehead seemed to be in a state of perpetual wrinkle. A long nose separated his rosy cheeks. A gray Vandyke beard circled his lips. His clear blue eyes embraced the young man with warmth.

The neophyte entered the room. He caught his breath. The walls were covered with Egyptian paintings. Vases and sculptures from the ancient civilization decorated the walls and furniture. The scent in the air was soft and pleasant, close to sandalwood. The visitor breathed deeply, then found his way to a stone seat. It was surprisingly comfortable.

His host sat on a similar seat and smiled. "Thank you for coming today, my friend. I'm the Director of Corporate Evolution. Do you know what that means?"

"Expanding and developing the corporation the same way you do your staff?"

The thin man smiled, his face lighting up. "You are an adept student. Just as the individual must coordinate and harmonize his mental functions, so must we coordinate and harmonize our corporate functions. This makes the organization run more efficiently, and helps us better relate to other businesses in the community."

The young man smiled. "You generate good will and it comes back to you. But...how do you deal with the many corporations that are run by sharks and cutthroats? Surely they don't share your beautiful ideals."

The voice was like a reed instrument, high and lofty, distant but near. "We either maneuver around them, or we don't deal with them. We must all learn to protect ourselves from selfish and predatory people. To do otherwise is self-destructive."

"I can see that."

"Further, we like to find honest and enterprising types like yourself and help them start their own businesses. This keeps our network of reliable contacts growing, and helps the cause of honest business in the world. We also create public charities and promote the health and well-being of the communities in which we thrive."

The visitor smiled knowingly. "And those acts of kindness and charity are doubled back to you many times over."

The gossamer eyes fluttered. "It is divinely selfish to give to others, for great rewards rebound from acts of charity and unselfish love. These rewards include expanded insight, intuition, greater will and better judgement in making decisions. When the mind is centered, it thinks most clearly. This is the antithesis to hostile competition - for when the conscious mind is filled with anxiety and fear, such higher connections are blocked. Charity and love open the door to incredibly creative and progressive thinking, allowing group intuition and problem-solving to flourish. This is the basis of *cooperative competition* and *win-win situations*, where everybody wins in a business deal."

"So if people truly try to work together, instead of sabotaging each other through warlike behavior, they can all benefit from their mutual skills and abilities."

"Yes. Rather than trying to consume one another like primitive animals in the jungle, people can ascend to a higher level of comprehension and functioning. This opens hearts and minds and allows them to work in concert with each other, rather than against one another. Everyone can benefit, which builds positive relations for future deals."

The young man vehemently shook his head. "It sounds so beautiful...but it reminds me of Sixties idealism. What about the law of the jungle...only the fittest survive?"

The forehead wrinkled, the Vandyke pursed. "There are many who are blind to the higher laws. They even seem to get away with it at times, but these periods are short-lived. There are those who start wars to make money, who appoint and puppeteer politicians, who control the media to control the mass mind. You've learned how people regularly hypnotize themselves with their illusional beliefs and fixated emotions - imagine what could happen if an entire nation...or an entire world were hypnotized by the media!"

The visitor's eyes became steely. He nodded. "There is much work to do. How can I help?"

The director beamed. "*Live the principles* you've been taught. Keep the light within, and fuel its flames with total love for yourself and all others. Realize that the power of the universe burns within each and every one of us, though few can see or feel it. It is like possessing the greatest treasure conceivable and not knowing it, preferring instead to worship a plastic ego or a worthless false belief. No, you must keep your heart pure and your mind clear, or else fall prey to illusion-makers and panderers."

"But how can you tell the difference?"

"By judgement, which comes from experience. Learn to trust people in slow degrees, taking nothing for granted. You don't want to block out the good people with distrust, but neither do you want to be used or hurt by liars and manipulators. So you give people a little rope at a time, and see what they do with it. If they prove trustworthy, give them a little more."

The young man nodded. "Rush into nothing. Being impulsive fosters self-destruction."

The executive smiled. "Exactly. Most importantly, teach these principles to others. To see life from a higher point of conscience fosters greater responsibility. And that is the keynote of the coming age - *personal responsibility*, for everything you think, feel, say and do."

The visitor was deep in thought as he walked to the door. He thanked the director profusely, studying the brilliant eyes burning beneath the pink forehead.

He again charged up the stairs, taking them several at a time. He stopped on the top landing, struck by a great realization.

He knew the secret of The Inner Manager.

Pausing for a moment on the landing, the young man wrote in his notebook, his hand shaking with excitement as he resolved to learn these ideas better than he had ever learned anything in his life:

<u>NOTES</u>

1. Corporations, like individuals, can create good will through selfless acts.

2. Charity and love return to one many times over, opening the doors to greater insight, intuition, will and judgement.

*3. **Cooperative competition** is based on **win-win situations**, which are fair and balanced for everyone involved. This eliminates warlike attitudes which only cause harm.*

4. To grow beyond the control of lower emotions, thereby discovering a higher state of conscience and will, is to assume greater responsibility for helping others.

CHANGE THE *LOWER* EMOTIONS

TO *HIGHER* EMOTIONS,

TO AVOID BEING

ENSLAVED

BY OTHER PEOPLE

ENLIGHTENMENT

The young man burst into the hallway on the top floor, eager to see the director of the corporation. He had many things to tell her.

She was waiting for him by her open door. Her face was perfect serenity. She somehow looked younger than she had earlier in the day. She led him into the room. She stood by the geodesic dome with the triangular top and looked deep into his eyes.

He nodded pleasantly, transfixed by the crystalline sparks of light streaming from her pupils. After a tranquil moment, she motioned for him to sit down.

"You are looking refreshed," she said. Her face was animated, the soft lines shifting and reforming around her delicate words. He could have sworn a faint glow enveloped her head and shoulders. It appeared to be golden on the outside, and became more violet closer to her body. Another time he might have shrugged it off, but not today.

He bowed gracefully. "I am profoundly in your debt. Today has been as instructive as it has been pleasurable."

Her eyes floated waves of warming light. "That is just as it should be. What have you learned?"

He took a deep breath and whistled. "I'll need a long period of time before I can fairly summarize."

She smiled knowingly. "Of course, but what stands out the most?"

He thought for a moment. "To begin with, we must distinguish illusion from reality. This can be difficult, because we often project what we think and feel onto the world around us. These projections reflect off the external world and return to us, giving us our perceptions. We must therefore be careful what we allow ourselves to think and feel, and refuse to allow irrational habits to dominate our minds. We must instead keep open, flexible minds, refusing to blind ourselves with misguided imagination."

The director beamed. "Excellent! You do learn fast. In fact, thoughts are created by the imagination, which combines emotional currents with the different forms of sensory stimuli, meaning sight, sound, touch, taste, smell, and the so-called *extrasensory* channels. These are little understood today, facts which many scientists prefer to deny and ignore since they can't yet explain the phenomena. In any case, emotions are often attached to certain thoughts by chance, depending on what you're feeling when the sensory imagery enters your system! Can you imagine...programming yourself to think and feel certain ways for years, based solely on chance and our lack of understanding about how the system works!"

The young man was incredulous. "I've been guilty of that, too..."

"So have we all, until we understand what we're doing to ourselves. Naturally, the thoughts and their attached emotions are stored in memory, arising again and again when set off by certain external or internal events."

The visitor interjected. "You mean they're like tapes which play over and over, repeating the same phrases with the same feelings, giving the person a sense of reality based only on familiarity and the self-fulfilling prophecy."

"Precisely! You can imagine what happens when we make a habit of feeling negative emotions. Negative leads to more negative, until the entire mind can be poisoned. We continue to create negative events and attract negative people to us...until we break those harmful cycles."

His interest was piqued. "How do we break those cycles?"

Warmth flowed from her. "One of the most powerful approaches is to change all your negative thinking and feeling into positive thinking and feeling the moment it starts. To do this, first tell yourself to be aware of all negative thinking and feeling as soon as it begins. Once you're aware of it happening, say to yourself, *STOP, I'M NOT GOING TO THINK THAT!* Then, replace the negative thought with two or more positive thoughts. For example, if you're angry at a friend and thinking nasty thoughts about that person, you can replace those thoughts by trying to understand the person's emotional problems, stress affecting the person, family difficulties and so on. Confront the person when you can about the problem, to resolve the conflict. Forgive them for what they did to you, and forgive yourself for your anger - but resolve to learn from that anger, to better handle such situations in the future."

The young man grinned. "You're saying turn off the tapes. Replace the negative thoughts with positive thoughts. Is it really that simple?"

Her smile was magnetic. "No. You must work hard to change your long-term habits of negative thought and emotion. You must resolve to remove from your person all negative feelings...the hurt, jealousy, anger, depression, guilt, anxiety...the whimpering, sniffling emotions you've collected over the years and stored away in your memory banks. All must be converted into love for yourself, love for others, and love for the greater force within."

The young man was deep in thought. "You mean love others no matter what they do, because it frees you from the chains of negative emotion..."

Her eyes sparkled from infinite shores. "Yes. Don't suppress your emotions, because that doesn't work. The emotions always come out somewhere. Instead, allow the emotional currents to rise, but change the direction and nature of the currents. For example, instead of being angry at someone, reframe how you see the situation, and find something good in it. Remember, all the negative feelings you hold inside primarily hurt yourself. If you gradually seed and fill your superconscious mind with only divine emotions, it gives you a tremendous power over life, for the higher frequencied energy of love dispels and untangles the lower frequencied energies of anger, fear, guilt and so on. Love frees your mind and allows you to transcend the petty illusions of this plane of potential pain."

"You mean take the emotional energy that's there and convert it into a positive force, a force that works for you, not against you."

"Exactly. What else must you do?"

He thought for a moment. "You must develop a powerfully positive self-image, one that bounces back no matter what negative garbage other people throw at you. The self-image is at the center of the cyclone, part of the nucleus of the system. If we maintain that positive self-image, we bring about positive effects in our lives, and in the lives of others."

She was radiant. "You are truly remarkable."

He glowed back at her. "It's like a boomerang, I guess...what we give off comes back to us. Probably to teach us the nature of ourselves and either the error...or the beauty...of our ways."

Somehow, her smile got brighter. "Please continue."

He let his thoughts play as his fingers came together to make a steeple. "There are many levels of consciousness, but we often fixate at a certain level due to our emotional habits. We must learn to break those negative fixations in order to recenter the mind, to return the conscious focus to the true center of the cyclone, the infinite nucleus within."

She nodded admiringly. "You have a natural comprehension of these ideas."

"Thank you," he blushed, before hurrying on. "We all have a responsibility to each other, so we must scrutinize our thoughts, feelings and actions to consider the effects they have on others. We must always do whatever produces the greatest good for the greatest number of people. Cooperation is far superior to cutthroat competition, because everyone can win. You can compete with yourself, to improve your own abilities. Competing with others is overrated in the marketplace. Cooperative thinking and the power of love expand your state of consciousness and your creative abilities."

Her eyes were shining like miniature suns. "Wonderful. Please go on."

"To improve our creative abilities, we must learn to concentrate and visualize properly, which includes observing the world closely and recreating the imagery during our visualization. We focus intensely on the things we want to happen, injecting feeling and sensory imagery. We then let go of it until the next visualization, while doing everything in our power physically to make it happen."

She was clearly impressed. "What else can we do?"

"We can develop our mental abilities by performing verbal and visual mental exercises, like crossword puzzles and playing chess. Combining verbal with visual improves memory. And we can program the superconscious mind to work for us - as we come into contact with it we discover the wellspring of creativity within. The imagination expands, allowing us to alter our referential fields of perception, by changing the underlying emotions and beliefs which anchor our minds into different levels of *reality.*"

She leaned forward, her body agile and youthful. Her glow seemed to fill the room. "I am proud to know you, my friend. Let these ideas sink to the depths of your mind, make them a part of your life. Practice these techniques and ideas, for they will set you free from the bonds that chain mankind to hopeless illusions. We are all meant to be free from these earthly irons, but we must first break the spell of negative emotions, of anger, rage, guilt, depression, anxiety and lust - so *beware of what you think about - your thoughts can turn into desires and fears.* For those who have the courage to make the transition, a new universe awaits within, a universe that transcends slavery to the material senses. A universe that few can imagine, a universe that exists in embryo within each of us. Greatness locked within, just a breath away."

The young man was speechless. He struggled to find his voice. "Who...who are you people? How can you know such things?"

Her smile was a portrait of beauty. "We know many unusual things. Each of us has been on the path for a long time, and our greatest love is to help others find the way to higher consciousness. The struggle is long and difficult, but the rewards are profound. We especially love to meet a person like yourself, one who opens and flowers before us, one who is ready for these ideas and who senses that far more exists beyond the mortal pale of madness that passes for normality."

He felt overwhelmed with wonder. "How can I ever thank you for these gifts of light?"

"Give them to others, that they might see. But only give it when asked, and only give as much as can be absorbed. Cast not your pearls before swine...remember...many marry in the mud."

He smiled gently. "May I introduce others to The Inner Manager?"

She laughed merrily, and he could have sworn that the sphere of light around her got brighter - but he couldn't be sure. "I see you've solved our little mystery."

He nodded as a crest of inspiration flooded his heart and mind. "The Inner Manager is the greater self within each of us, the *superconscious sun* that fills our lives with wonder and brilliance...if we but allow it. It is what Freud meant by the subconscious mind, but it is much more than he dared imagine. It is the nucleus of the atom of consciousness, the positive center of our minds about which spin electrons of thought that we create in response to our emotions and sensory information. Our emotions rise like magnetic fields from that nucleus, holding the electrons of thought in place. We are each a universe within, and that is humankind's *final frontier...inner space.*"

Her eyes became flames of energy burning into his brows. The globe of light about her head and shoulders seemed to grow until it embraced the entire room. He felt a sense of heat, then light flooded his mind with a kaleidoscope of images. He was carried away by lilting visions, to lands he had never dreamed possible.

Somewhere in flight, he heard her melodic voice intone, "Thank you, great friend, for having graced us with your presence today. We hope you are now ready to begin your own business...or, you might wish to join us here..."

The young man breathed long, deep breaths, the elixir of energy filling his lungs and heart and mind.

He had never felt better in his life.

The young man left the building on a cloud of peace and contentment. He paused in the middle of the sidewalk and made his notes, unmindful of the crowds passing by. He was determined to study the notes for the rest of his life:

<u>NOTES</u>

1. To distinguish illusion from reality, we must keep open, flexible minds and be aware of how we connect our thoughts and emotions together. We can change these connections at will, using repetition of new linkages, in concert with imagination and determination.

2. We must maintain a powerfully positive self-image in order to attract positive circumstances in our lives, and to counteract the negativities of others.

*3. We create our own level of consciousness with our thought-emotion fixations, giving us our unique referential fields of perception and producing our daily **realities.***

4. These thought-emotion fixations project our intentions, desires and fears into the surrounding world and eventually make either our desires - or fears - come true.

*5. We are each responsible for every thought, emotion and action we take, and must therefore learn to direct our actions toward helping others and toward the greatest good for all, or else suffer the reflective consequences. **The higher level our understanding attains, the more severe will those consequences be.***

6. We become what we feel, in the shape and form of what we think.

7. We must develop all our mental functions, which helps bring the superconscious and conscious minds into better contact.

8. We are each born to be free, not shackled by the emotional prisons engendered by ourselves or others.

*9. **The Inner Manager** is the higher self within, our fountain of life and wellspring of creativity. It but awaits our attention and development to be born into our lives...*

THE

POWER

OF MIND

APPROACHES

INFINITY

WHEN

LOVE

FILLS THE

HEART

References

Barron, F., & Harrington, D.M. (1981). Creativity, intelligence, and personality. Annual Review of Psychology, 32, 439-476.

Blanchard, K., & Johnson, S. (1982). The one minute manager. New York: Berkley Books.

Busse, T.V., & Mansfield, R.S. (1980). Theories of the creative process: A review and a perspective. Journal of Creative Behavior, 14(2), 91-103; 132.

Carnegie, D. (1981). How to win friends and influence people (rev. ed.). New York: Pocket Books.

Cohen, L.W., & Ehrlich, G. (1963). The structure of the real number system. Princeton, NJ: D. Van Nostrand Co., Inc.

Corsini, R.J. & Contributors. (1979). Current psychotherapies. Itasca, IL: F.E. Peacock Publishers, Inc.

Dalrymple, R. (1985). Increase your power of creative thinking in eight days. San Jose, CA: Amorc Publishing, Inc.

DeBono, E. (1967). The five day course in thinking. New York: Basic Books.

Einstein, A. (1961). Relativity: The special and the general theory (R. Lawson, Trans.). New York: Bonanza Books.

Erickson, M.H. (1969). A special inquiry with Aldous Huxley into the nature and character of various states of consciousness. In C.T. Tart (Ed.), Altered states of consciousness. New York: Wiley.

Frank, J.D. (1974). Persuasion and healing. New York: Schocken Books.

Freud, S. (1952). On dreams (James Strachey, Trans.). New York: W.W. Norton & Company, Inc. (Original work published 1901)

Freud, S. (1958). On creativity and the unconscious. New York: Harper & Row. (Original work published 1925)

Freud, S. (1960). The psychopathology of everyday life (Alan Tyson, Trans.). New York: W.W. Norton & Company, Inc. (Original work published 1901)

Gendlin, E. (1969). Focusing. Psychotherapy: Theory, Research and Practice, 6, 4-15.

Glover, J.A. (1977). Risky shift and creativity. Social Behavior and Personality, 5(2), 317-320.

Gordon, W.J.J. (1961). Synectics. New York: Harper.

Greenson, R.R. (1967). The technique and practice of psychoanalysis (Vol. 1). New York: International Universities Press, Inc.

Guilford, J.P. (1957). Creative abilities in the arts. Psychological Review, 64, 110-118.

Hadramard, J. (1945). The psychology of invention in the mathematical field. Princeton: Princeton University Press.

Hummel, J.A. (1967). Introduction to vector functions. Reading, MA: Addison-Wesley.

Jones, E. (1953). The life and work of Sigmund Freud (Vol. 1). New York: Basic Books.

Jung, C.G. (1974). Dreams (R.F.C. Hull, Trans.). Princeton, NJ: Princeton University Press.

Kubie, L.S. (1958). Neurotic distortions of the creative process. Lawrence, KS: University of Kansas Press.

Kuhn, T.S. (1970). The structure of scientific revolutions (2nd ed.), 2(2). Chicago: The University of Chicago.

Lorayne, H. (1985). Page-A-Minute memory book. New York: Holt, Rinehart and Winston.

Mandino, O. (1968). The greatest salesman in the world. New York: Bantam Books.

Maslow, K. (1959). Creativity in self-actualizing people. In H. Anderson (Ed.), Creativity and its cultivation. New York: Harper.

Meichenbaum, D. (1975). Enhancing creativity by modifying what subjects say to themselves. American Educational Research Journal, 12(2), 129-145.

Moise, E. (1967). Calculus. Reading, MA: Addison-Wesley Publishing Company.

Mueller, L.K. (1978). Beneficial and detrimental modeling effects on creative response production. The Journal of Psychology, 98, 253-260.

Osborn, A.F. (1963). Applied imagination (3rd ed.). New York: Scribner & Sons.

Ouspensky, P.D. (1982). Tertium organum (E. Kadloubovsky, Trans.). New York: Vintage Books. (Original work published 1922)

Parnes, S.J. (1967). Creative behavior guidebook. New York: Scribner & Sons.

Patterson, C.H. (1986). Theories of counseling and psychotherapy (4th ed.). New York: Harper & Row.

Powell, J. (1974). The secret of staying in
love. Allen, TX: Argus Communications.

Prince, G.M. (1970). The practice of creativity.
New York: Harper.

Rimm, D.C., & Masters, J.C. (1979). Behavior
therapy: Techniques and empirical findings
(2nd ed.). New York: Academic Press.

Robinson, D. (1981). An intellectual history of
psychology. New York: Macmillan.

Sims, B.T. (1976). Fundamentals of topology.
New York: Macmillan.

Stein, M.I. (1974). Stimulating creativity
(Vol. 1). New York: Academic Press.

Stein, M.I. (1975). Stimulating creativity
(Vol. 2). New York: Academic Press.

Torrance, E.P. (1962). Guiding creative talent.
Englewood Cliffs, NJ: Prentice-Hall.

Vick, J.W. (1973). Homology theory: An
introduction to algebraic topology. San
Diego, CA: Academic Press.

Walkup, L.E. (1965). Creativity in science
through visualization. Perceptual and
Motor Skills, 21, 35-41.

Wallas, G. (1926). The art of thought. New
York: Harcourt.

Wiener, N. (1961). <u>Cybernetics: or control and communication in the animal and the machine</u> (2nd ed.). Cambridge, MA: The M.I.T. Press.

INCREASE YOUR POWER OF CREATIVE THINKING IN EIGHT DAYS !

Have you ever felt stymied, locked-up inside and unable to truly express yourself? Do you ever feel down on yourself or others, falling into cycles of negative thought and feeling?

"Negative thoughts and feelings," stated Dr. Ron Dalrymple in a recent interview, "greatly limit our ability to solve problems and to attain success and happiness in life. By learning how to develop a powerfully positive self-image and by tapping the power of the inner mind, most people can unleash talents and abilities currently dormant inside them."

Dr. Dalrymple's book, *Increase Your Power of Creative Thinking in Eight Days!* (ISBN 0-912057-41-6; LCC No. 85-50428) is based on research conducted at the University of Maryland. Organized into an eight day program for ease of learning, the book teaches three mind-stimulating approaches to creative thinking: the first shows you how to tap the power of the inner mind and develop a creative self-image; the second teaches you how to understand problems and the world around you in many new, creative ways; and the third teaches you to put these techniques to practice in your daily life.

A licensed psychologist and creativity expert, Dr. Ron Dalrymple is a member of the American Psychological Association, the Maryland Psychological Association, the National Register of Health Service Providers in Psychology, MENSA, Phi Beta Kappa, Phi Kappa Phi and Psi Chi Honorary Fraternities.

Please see reverse side of page to order this book.

ORDER FORM

Celestial Gifts Publishing
Post Office Box 414-0001
Chester, MD 21619
Telephone (301) 643-4466

Please send me the following books by Dr. Ron Dalrymple:

Quantity   <u>Totals</u>

_____ *The Inner Manager* @$8.95 each = _____

_____ *Increase Your Power of Creative Thinking in Eight Days* @$14.95 each = _____

Subtotal   = _____

Maryland: Please add 5% sales tax   = _____

Shipping: $1.00 for the first book and $.50 for each additional book   = _____

I can't wait 3-4 weeks for Book Rate. Here is $3.00 per book for Air Mail   = _____

Final Total   = _____

Name: _____
Address: _____
_____ ZIP: _____

I understand that I may return any book for a full refund if not satisfied.

INCREASE YOUR POWER OF CREATIVE THINKING IN EIGHT DAYS !

Have you ever felt stymied, locked-up inside and unable to truly express yourself? Do you ever feel down on yourself or others, falling into cycles of negative thought and feeling?

"Negative thoughts and feelings," stated Dr. Ron Dalrymple in a recent interview, "greatly limit our ability to solve problems and to attain success and happiness in life. By learning how to develop a powerfully positive self-image and by tapping the power of the inner mind, most people can unleash talents and abilities currently dormant inside them."

Dr. Dalrymple's book, *Increase Your Power of Creative Thinking in Eight Days!* (ISBN 0-912057-41-6; LCC No. 85-50428) is based on research conducted at the University of Maryland. Organized into an eight day program for ease of learning, the book teaches three mind-stimulating approaches to creative thinking: the first shows you how to tap the power of the inner mind and develop a creative self-image; the second teaches you how to understand problems and the world around you in many new, creative ways; and the third teaches you to put these techniques to practice in your daily life.

A licensed psychologist and creativity expert, Dr. Ron Dalrymple is a member of the American Psychological Association, the Maryland Psychological Association, the National Register of Health Service Providers in Psychology, MENSA, Phi Beta Kappa, Phi Kappa Phi and Psi Chi Honorary Fraternities.

Please see reverse side of page to order this book.

ORDER FORM

Celestial Gifts Publishing
Post Office Box 414-0001
Chester, MD 21619
Telephone (301) 643-4466

Please send me the following books by Dr. Ron Dalrymple:

Quantity   Totals
_____ *The Inner Manager* @$8.95 each =_____

_____ *Increase Your Power of Creative Thinking in Eight Days* @$14.95 each = _____

Subtotal   = _____

Maryland: Please add 5% sales tax   = _____

Shipping: $1.00 for the first book and $.50 for each additional book   = _____

I can't wait 3-4 weeks for Book Rate. Here is $3.00 per book for Air Mail   = _____

Final Total   = _____

Name: _____
Address: _____
_____ ZIP: _____

I understand that I may return any book for a full refund if not satisfied.